Into the Wild:
Family Micro Adventures
The Pocket Guide

Claire Pinder

In loving memory of my boys' father Stephen

A free spirit, forever in our hearts

1984–2021

Table of Contents

About the Author

Claire is a working mum and solo parent to two boys. She studied Primary School Teaching but spent most of her career working in People and Talent teams and delivering training programs in the high-tech industry. Growing up in West Berkshire, the local woods were her playground for adventuring with friends. Her parents instilled a love for the outdoors and exploration from a young age, taking the family on varied adventures, including UK camping holidays, cycling expeditions, water sports tuition in the Cotswolds and annual hiking trips in Wales.

In 2023, Claire took a break from her career to explore her passion for the outdoors and trained as an outdoor survival instructor. Claire hopes this book will inspire others to embrace more outdoor adventures and aims to shed light on the health and child development benefits of getting out into nature.

With Thanks

To my family, especially…

For my incredible boys, Lachlan and Elias,
My adventure team
My everything
Run until you fly!

With love and special thanks to Mum and Dad
My inspiration to live adventurously
You make my world shine brighter every day!

Some Further Thanks

A book is never one person's journey; it requires help, support, and encouragement from others.

Thank you to:

Bonnie Craig for her brilliance in editing and all her help, advice, and guidance to finalise this book.

Helen Polden and Andy Meaden for bringing the adventures to life with beautiful illustrations.

All my friends and family who showed encouragement and support throughout and who believed I was able to write a book.

Dawny for listening, caring, and championing me on every step of the way x

I Give to You

This book is your pocket guide of ideas for outdoor mini or micro adventures with children and the special people in your life. I hope this gives you inspiration and a spark to take action, as well as practical tips and advice for planning outdoor family adventures and making more memories together in the wild.

The book presents everything you need to prepare for a mini expedition. You will discover the value of curiosity, being open to new experiences, and finding delight in creating lasting memories in nature with your family. It also provides insights into the many benefits for the body, mind, and soul and for your child's development.

Whether you regularly enjoy and embark on family outdoor adventures, dip into these very occasionally, or are a self-confessed techy and love staying in the warm at home, this book is designed to inspire anyone.

I ask only that you consider any adjustments required to suit your family's needs, abilities, and interests or to better suit your local surroundings, wherever you live on this awesome planet!

So, prepare to move outside your comfort zone, and get ready to embark on beautiful experiences, no matter how small.

Let your imagination run wild!

A mind that is stretched by a new experience can never go back to its old dimensions.

– Oliver Wendell Holmes

What are Family Micro Adventures?

Family micro adventures are mini outdoor experiences or expeditions for adults/parents and children. They are fun for everyone, affordable, often close to home, and can be squeezed into your weekends or evenings.

The idea is to take everyone away from routine and to make the most of the world outside.

Why this book? Planning adventures or thinking up ideas in our busy lives can be tricky. Too often, we find ourselves plugging back into tech or tackling the never-ending to-do list because we haven't come up with that perfect idea in the moment. Another week slips by, and life starts to lack a bit of excitement. Frankly, it can all look a bit repetitive.

The challenge of coming up with ideas and turning them into action got me thinking. Like a cookbook when I need inspiration for a family dinner, I wanted a guidebook full of ideas for getting outdoors and having new adventures. The obvious place to start was my little bedside notebook. Over the years, I've jotted down ideas and experiences we've had as a family, and it's become my go-to list to browse over with a cup of coffee on a Saturday morning when I'm looking for inspiration.

That notebook is now this book, with some extras added and a tidy-up!

The ideas for family micro adventures in this book have been organised into seven sections. Each adventure has information on what age it is suitable for, how to prepare, the best locations to head to, and what kit you will need.

What are the Benefits?

There are many good reasons to break from routine and embark on an adventure.

The outdoors is a gift with a huge amount to offer us if we find ways to make the most of it. Some of the better-known advantages include being active, filling our lungs with fresh air, and gaining new experiences that give us energy and make us feel alive. Being outside has a unique way of balancing our mental state with both excitement and a sense of calm and purpose.

For our minds, micro adventures are like brain superpowers. They help you think creatively, solve challenges, and boost your self-esteem. When you try something new, such as climbing a tree or kayaking down a river, your brain becomes excited and develops new abilities. You're giving your brain a workout.

Here are a few more reasons to embrace the outdoors.

- Create new, unique experiences to bond as a family.

- Take a break from busy, stressful routines and daily life.

- Connect with nature and discover its beauty.

- Disconnect from tech.

- Reduce your carbon footprint.

- Learn life skills, and create opportunities to be curious.

- Boost your immune system and soak up vitamin D.

- Improve mental health with serotonin.

Spending time outdoors also plays an important role in a child's development. Engaging in outdoor adventures can help reduce anxiety and behavioural issues. These experiences can also help to build a child's resilience and curiosity, strengthen family relationships, boost self-confidence, help to develop problem-solving abilities, and improve collaboration skills. They can even help with academic performance and provide opportunities for adults to model positive parenting behaviours and respect for the world around them.

During childhood, our developing brains are heavily influenced by the experiences we have. Environmental factors and families play a central role in early years development. If we help to lay solid foundations, we support positive brain development.

A research study published in *Environment and Behaviour*[1] found that nearly all adults listed the outdoors as the most significant place during their childhood. The researchers explained that developing all our senses is a foundational experience in childhood, tying it strongly to memory.

If we go back a hundred years, or even just a few decades, children were often free to play and explore their local wilderness, from fields to farms to woodland, with little or no supervision. Since the urbanisation of the last century, many children now grow up in built-up environments where access to and regular connection with nature has significantly reduced. Yet numerous studies have highlighted the importance of the outdoors and nature for positive child development.

Research published in 2017 in the *Journal of Environmental Psychology*[2] studied 562 Norwegian preschoolers for four consecutive years. They found that children who spent more hours outdoors scored higher on cognitive tests, had improved memory and showed less inattention-hyperactivity symptoms than students who spent fewer hours outdoors.

With so many known benefits, let's get our minds ready for living more adventurously and stepping into the wild. As Jimmy Chan, a professional athlete, film director and author said, "As human beings we have an innate need to explore, to see what's around the corner."[3]

References

[1] Bento, G. & Dias, G. (2017). The importance of outdoor play for young children's healthy development. *Porto Biomedical Journal*, 2(5), 157–160.

[2] Ulset, V., Vitaro, F., Brendgen, M., Bekkhus, M., & Borge, A. I. H. (2017) Time spent outdoors during preschool: Links with children's cognitive and behavioral development. *Journal of Environmental Psychology*, 52, 69–80.

[3] Synnott, M. (2015) Adventure filmmaker Jimmy Chin talks risk, fatherhood, and fame. *National Geographic*. www.nationalgeographic.com/adventure/article/meru-filmmaker-jimmy-chin-opens-up-about-his-life-on-the-edge-video-exclusive

Don't Hold Back, Be Curious, Let's Do This!

Here are some tips to get your mind and body ready.

- **Be open to new experiences**: To encourage curiosity and spontaneity, begin by being open to new experiences. Accept the unknown and be willing to venture outside your comfort zone.

- **Follow your instincts**: Listen to your intuition and trust your instincts when selecting micro adventures. If anything catches your eye or sparks your curiosity, go for it!

- **Embrace the element of surprise**: Make room for surprises and unexpected discoveries on your mini trips. Instead of exhaustively arranging every detail, leave some elements open-ended. Accept the volatility and let the adventure unfold.

- **Investigate your local area**: Curiosity begins at home. Take some time to look around your local area with new eyes. Look for new parks, trails, or landmarks close to home. Approach familiar sites with curiosity, and you could be surprised by the unique sensations and viewpoints you encounter.

- **Engage your surroundings**: During your micro excursions, use all of your senses to immerse yourself in the current moment. Take in the sights, sounds, and fragrances around you. Engaging with your environment will help you appreciate each experience more.

- **Ask questions and be open to learning**: Curiosity thrives on information, so ask lots of questions. Seek information and learn about the areas you visit. Engage with locals, examine informational signs, or conduct some preliminary research.

- **Document and reflect**: Capture the experiences and memories of your trips through photography, writing, or simply taking mental notes. Later, take some time to reflect on your experiences. What did you find out? What surprised you? What did you learn? Reflection will strengthen your connection to the trip.

Remember that embracing the attitude of getting started is about being open-minded, following your intuition, and connecting with the environment. Step out, explore, and allow your curiosity to lead you to unique, unplanned experiences!

Into the Wild

Admire the Sunrise

Set the alarm clock for an hour before sunrise, and head out to a nearby hilltop. Entice the family with bacon butties, chopped fresh fruit, coffee, and a flask of hot chocolate. You won't forget the experience.

> Planning: Not much
>
> Age: All ages
>
> Location: Somewhere high up or where you can see the horizon (remember to face east, where the sun rises from)
>
> Time: 2–3 hours
>
> Kit list: Alarm clock, comfortable clothing, warm layers, walking shoes, water bottle, snacks, camera or smartphone, journal and pen, blanket, headlamp or torch, insect repellent or waterproofs (if needed)

This early-rise adventure is about experiencing the beauty and tranquillity of the early morning hours and taking a moment to appreciate the sun. It entails getting up before daybreak to see the planet awaken. By immersing yourself in the peace of the early morning, you can energise your body and gain a deeper appreciation for the world around you. Children love the excitement of getting up in the early hours, and best of all, everyone can stay in their pyjamas and take a favourite blanket to keep off the morning chill.

Tip: Show children how to use the sun for navigation. Once the sun has risen and is in view, all you need for this wilderness survival hack is an analogue watch set to the correct time. If you are in the northern hemisphere, hold your watch flat on the palm of your hand, and point the hour hand in the direction of the sun. Bisect the angle between the hour hand and 12 o'clock to find south. Before noon, measure clockwise from the hour hand to the 12 o'clock marking, while in the afternoon, measure counterclockwise from the hour hand to 12 o'clock.

For example, if it's 5 o'clock in the afternoon and you've lined up your hour hand with the sun, south is the direction exactly between the 2 and 3 o'clock marks, and north is the spot across from this point. Note that during daylight saving time, you must use 1 o'clock instead 12 o'clock.

Nature Hunt and Discovery Hike

This mini adventure is perfect for a weekend, mid-week evening or even to add some fun to a dog walk. A nature hunt awakens the senses and helps to lift energy levels by giving the experience more purpose and a goal to focus on. So assemble your fellow nature enthusiasts, grab your hunting gear, and start on a discovery trip among the beauties of the great outdoors.

Planning: Not much

Age: All ages

Location: Woods, parks, hills – anywhere!

Time: 1–2 hours

Kit list: Backpack, map and compass, items list and a pen for each group, snacks, water bottle, weather-appropriate clothing, insect repellent and sunscreen (if needed), camera, comfy footwear, watch or phone

Before heading out, pick an area you can explore and make a list of natural items you will likely find in the area, such as pine cones, types of trees or leaves, animal footprints, feathers, types of rock, flowers, etc. Share the list of items with the group and decide whether to go as one group or to split up, depending on age, ability, and group size. Agree when you will meet back at the starting point to share your finds.

Gather everyone for a debrief once the teams have completed their quest or reached a set time limit. Allow each team to discuss their experiences, share pictures of their findings, and describe any intriguing observations they made along the way. You can finish the adventure by offering an award to the team that finds the most items from the list in the agreed time frame or simply recognise everyone's involvement.

Beach Vibes and Sand Sculpture Competition

This fun, beach-themed adventure promotes creativity and problem-solving skills. If you work in pairs, it will also help to foster collaboration and conflict resolution.

Planning: Not much

Age: All ages

Location: Seaside or city beach

Time: 2 hours

Kit list: Buckets and spades, clothing and footwear to suit the weather, sun protection, water bottle, snacks

Safety: Keep an eye on children at all times.

With minimal planning required, except for checking the weather and deciding on the location, you can embark on a fun-filled adventure. You don't need hot weather; just decide if you need beach hats and sunscreen or wellies and raincoats. Let the children's imagination take the lead in deciding the theme for the sand sculptures, from sea creatures, to castles, dinosaurs, and beyond. Agree a time limit, set the rules (e.g., collecting and using natural items found on the beach to decorate sculptures), find your own spot, and start building your sand sculpture. At the end of the time limit, you could ask a passer-by to assess the sculptures' ingenuity, creativity, and overall aesthetic appeal. Don't forget to take pictures before you finish and leave no trace by returning natural items to where you found them.

If you have more time available, you can play other games, such as a beach treasure hunt: give the children a list of items to find and set the timer. Take boules, roll down sand dunes, or play tug of war using a skipping rope. Tip: Prepare snacks with the children before you set off. Sausage or sweet potato and feta rolls are simple and quick to make, and you can adapt the fillings to suit the family.

Nature Artwork

Go foraging in local parks or woodland to collect and create your natural artwork. You can create your picture while on your walk, once you get home, or save creating your artwork for a rainy day.

Planning: Not much

Age: All ages

Location: Any natural setting such as local parks, woodland, hills, beaches, etc.

Time: As long as you fancy!

Kit list: Nature reference books, portable easel or surface, sketchbook, pencils, snacks, water bottle, sunscreen and insect repellent (depending on location), comfortable clothing and footwear

This adventure is all about getting creative and the reward at the end once you produce your artwork inspired by what you discovered. You can choose to forage and collect items from the ground (remember to avoid picking anything), while being mindful of local laws on foraging, which can easily be found online. Take a book to identify wildflowers if you have one.

Whether you're an accomplished artist or love exploring your artistic side, this micro adventure allows you to express your creativity and take inspiration from nature. Observing and interpreting natural aspects into a visual representation can be soothing and gratifying, allowing everyone to connect more with the natural world.

Children may prefer to forage and create their masterpieces using paints and glue at home. Create a frame out of sticks and find a perfect spot to hang it on the wall to enjoy for years to come.

Tip: Leaf rubbing artworks are easy to create with younger children. You can do these with paper and crayons or pencils while on your adventure. Place a leaf beneath a sheet of paper and wipe a crayon or pencil over the surface to capture the intricacies and textures of the leaf. Find leaves in varying shapes, sizes, and textures to create your masterpiece.

Step Back in Time

History is everywhere, and there's a vast amount of sites you can visit for little to no cost. Seek out lesser-known historic sites online to plan where to go, and see if there's anywhere close to home that you can reach on foot or by bike.

> Planning: Medium
>
> Age: All ages
>
> Location: Places of historic significance
>
> Time: Make it a day trip
>
> Kit list: Suitable clothing for the weather, water bottle, snacks, camera or smartphone, guidebook, notepad and pen, cash or cards (for admission fees, etc.)

A historic site allows you to dive into the past and can be a great opportunity to learn and be curious. There's plenty to see, from castles to ruins, monuments, or landmarks. Locals may be able to share fascinating stories, so be bold and ask! Discover architectural marvels, study historical treasures, and engage in activities that bring history to life.

Go Fly a Kite

The perfect activity for a windy day! Flying kites is fun for everyone, and if you head up a nearby hill, you'll likely find others making the most of the windy weather and creating a colourful display in the sky.

Planning: Medium

Age: All ages

Location: Up high!

Time: 1–2 hours

Kit list: Kite, kite string, kite tail, picnic blanket, sunscreen, hat, water bottle, snacks

Find a hill or open area with plenty of space for kite flying. Bring a kite and basic items like a spool of thread and a picnic blanket. When you reach the hill, unfold your kite, secure the line, and let the wind lift it into the sky. Kite flying takes teamwork, so help each other to get your kite soaring in the sky. Take a minute to observe the surroundings and breathe in some fresh air.

Tip: While you are out, why not build a wind chime? You can easily do this with sticks, string, and a collection of natural items. Have a look online for ideas for natural wind chimes, and together practise tying a fisherman's knot to secure everything.

Seek Out Minibeasts

Observing and appreciating the vast diversity of insects is a fascinating adventure, perfect for younger children. You may want to take a notepad and pen to jot down or draw what you find. Alternatively, take photos to identify what you found online once you get home from your exploration.

Planning: Not much

Age: All ages

Location: Woods, parks, gardens, coastlines, etc.

Time: 1–2 hours

Kit list: Magnifying glass, pen and paper, local insect book, camera or smartphone, binoculars, weather-appropriate clothing, water bottle, snacks, sunhat, insect repellent and sunscreen (if needed)

Pick a location where insects are likely to thrive, such as a walking trail, garden, or woodland. Look around for any movement or evidence of insect activity: search plants, flowers, trees, and the ground to see what you can find. To see more detail, use a magnifying glass or a camera with a macro lens.

Respecting the insects and their environment is critical: avoid handling or disturbing them. Remember to admire these small organisms' intricate beauty and value in the environment. This adventure allows you to engage with nature on a smaller scale while also developing a greater knowledge of and respect for the frequently ignored world of insects. If you can, take a book on local insects to help identify what you find.

Outdoor Adventure Sports

On Your Bike!

Get onto your saddle and explore bike trails or cycle tracks in your local area. Old railway lines that have been turned into bike trails are fantastic for easy, safe cycling routes, so find out if there are any nearby. For the more adventurous adrenaline seekers, find a local pump track!

Planning: Medium

Age: All ages (bike trailers or attachments can be used for younger children)

Location: Woods, parks, bike trails, pump tracks, local cycle routes

Time: Half a day

Kit list: Bike, helmet, water bottle, snacks, puncture repair kit, map, sunscreen, sunglasses, comfortable clothing, appropriate footwear, first aid kit

Exploring your surroundings while enjoying the thrill of cycling is a great way to get outdoors with children. Begin by researching local bike trails or pump tracks suitable for various skill levels. Whether you prefer a leisurely ride through picturesque landscapes or a more challenging route, or if you're an adrenaline seeker looking for a pump track, there's something for everyone.

Once you've decided on the right path, prepare your bikes and appropriate supplies. Before starting, check the weather forecast and make sure everyone's bikes are operating well.

If you have young children, consider using bike trailers or attachments for a safe and enjoyable experience. If you don't have these, look for local bike rental centres that rent these.

Once you're on your bike, take in the views and sounds as you ride along the track. Plan a few rest stops to enjoy the landscape, or bring a picnic to have at a scenic location on the route.

Tip: If you want to keep close to home and don't have much time to spare, you could cycle to a nearby letterbox to post some letters or to a local shop to grab an ice cream.

Get Physical with a Family Triathlon

A family triathlon typically consists of three activities: swimming, cycling, and running. It's an opportunity to push yourselves, encourage one another, and celebrate your accomplishments as a family.

> Planning: Medium
>
> Age: 5+
>
> Location: Parks, lakes, lidos, outdoor pools
>
> Time: Half a day
>
> Kit list: Bikes, bike attachments (if needed), swimwear, towels, running shoes, helmets, water bottles, snacks, sunscreen, sunglasses, comfortable clothing, first aid kit, puncture repair kit

Choose an appropriate site near a swimming pool or a lake that allows public swimming. Look for nearby cycle routes and jogging trails to complete the triathlon course. Remember to select distances that are appropriate for everyone's fitness levels and ages. If you are swimming in a lake, you may want to take wetsuits, and you will need life jackets. For pool swimming, children may require buoyancy aids. This activity is perfect for inviting others along, and you could celebrate finishing the triathlon together with a BBQ. Note, never swim alone, and make sure everyone is a confident swimmer. You can adjust the sports; for instance, you can replace swimming with an egg and spoon race, skipping, or kayaking. Safety is key for this one, so make sure everyone's confident with the sports you choose, you have the right gear, and children are always with an adult.

Slacklining

Slacklining is a brilliant sport for strengthening your core and improving your balance. You'll need a slackline, but luckily it's not a costly item. You also need enough space – you could use your garden, woods, or a local park.

Planning: Medium

Age: 6+

Location: Fields, park, garden, woods

Time: 1–2 hours

Kit list: Slackline with ratchets, tree protectors, comfortable clothing, shoes with good grip, first aid kit, water bottles

Slacklining involves balancing and walking along a tight line, usually secured between two large trees or solid poles. It provides a fun and challenging experience for people of all fitness levels. First, choose a good place with two strong anchor points and enough room to set up the line. Ensure the anchor points can support the weight and stress of the slackline.

For safety, it's best to set up the slackline low to the ground; about half a metre is plenty. There's a bit of a technique to this one, so a great way to start would be to watch a video online before you head out. Time how long each person can stay on the line and help younger ones get up and balance if needed.

Go for a Hike

Hiking is an energising and gratifying micro adventure that allows you to immerse yourself in the vast outdoors and enjoy time in the wilderness. Choose a hiking location and route that meets your group's fitness levels. Investigate local routes, national parks, or nature reserves in your region, and choose a trail that provides the appropriate amount of challenge for your group. Consider mileage, elevation gain, and any unique points of interest.

Planning: Medium

Age: All ages

Location: Hilly regions, mountains, rivers, nature reserves

Time: Half a day or a day

Kit list: Backpack, hiking boots or trainers, comfortable clothing, water bottle, snacks, navigation tools (map, compass, GPS), sunscreen, insect repellent, first aid kit, rain gear (if necessary), headlamp or torch, multi-tool, whistle, emergency blanket, litter picker handle and bag

A family hike can be the perfect opportunity for some spontaneity and to dial up the excitement levels for everyone. Try letting the children take the lead and decide which trail to take or whether to turn left or right so long as the area is safe enough to do so. Keep an eye on your food and water levels and when you need to start heading back.

It's definitely worth taking a picnic if you are going out for a few hours. Having enough water is key, so make sure everyone is carrying at least one bottle. It's also a great opportunity to do some litter picking on the route to make it a more rewarding challenge and to be more environmentally responsible.

Head Out of Your Back Door

Garden Assault Course

Transforming your garden or outdoor space into an obstacle course is a simple yet incredibly enjoyable adventure. It's an opportunity to push yourself physically, create some healthy competition, and use your imagination to design your course.

Planning: Medium

Age: 5+

Location: Garden or local park

Time: 2 hours

Kit list: Ropes, tyres, poles, cones, buckets, planks, tarpaulin, markers, timer, water bottles, snacks, anything you can find to design your course!

To make a garden assault course, first design a sequence of obstacles and challenges using items from your garden or home. Set up a balance beam made from a fallen tree limb, make a crawling tunnel out of cardboard boxes, lay stepping stones made of pebbles or logs, hang ropes or ribbons for players to walk through – the possibilities are endless.

Ask each child to design a couple of obstacles, or work in pairs depending on numbers. Half the fun is setting up the course. Think about the different ages and how to adapt to keep it fair, for example, depending on age and ability, deduct minutes from their overall time or put out ribbons to collect along the route instead of timing everyone.

Giant Games

Using chalk, you can transform a garden patio or outdoor space into larger-than-life classic board games such as Connect 4, Noughts and Crosses, and Snakes and Ladders.

Planning: Not much

Age: All ages

Location: Parks, garden patio, paths

Time: 1–2 hours

Kit list: Chalk, dice, rocks, sticks, water bottle, appropriate clothing and footwear

Find a suitable location, such as a garden patio, driveway, or pavement. For Connect 4, draw six rows and seven columns. Ask participants to find 15–20 leaves of the same type as their markers. Make sure each person collects a different type of leaf.

Draw a meandering path with numbered squares using chalk for Snakes and Ladders. Draw snakes and ladders along the path to indicate where players will travel ahead or backwards, depending on the square they land on. Players take turns rolling dice and moving their game pieces along the course, attempting to cross the finish line first.

Create a Mini Garden

This adventure gives children autonomy and ownership over what they create and an opportunity to nurture their garden over time. From a mini garden to a larger vegetable patch, choose what will work for your space, whether it is a garden, balcony, or even a large plant pot or old welly boot.

Planning: Medium

Age: All ages

Location: Garden, balcony

Time: 2–3 hours

Kit list: Planting pots or containers, soil, seeds or seedlings, watering can or hose, gardening tools (trowel, hand rake, etc.). Optional: fertilizer or compost

Select a good spot with ample sunshine and prepare the soil by cleaning and loosening any debris. Consider using containers or raised beds if you have limited room. Choose the plants or veggies you wish to grow. Plant the seeds or seedlings according to the instructions.

Mini gardens can be decorated with items such as stones or by making colourful garden windmills using paper, straws, scissors, a pin, and paint or crayons to decorate.

Spring is ideal for this adventure as most seeds are recommended to be sown at this time of year.

Build a Fairy House

This can be rewarding and enjoyable for younger children and a great outdoor activity to do in your garden or a local park. It can also be built in a large plant pot indoors if you don't have the outside space.

Planning: Medium

Age: All ages

Location: Garden, parks

Time: 2–3 hours

Kit list: Natural materials such as twigs, leaves, rocks, and pinecones, craft supplies like glue, string, and small decorative items, scissors or pruning shears, container or base for the fairy house. Optional: fairy figurines or small toys, paint or markers for decorating, fairy-themed books or stories for inspiration

Find an area in your garden or a local park with natural materials such as twigs, leaves, and moss. Build your fairy house using your ideas and ingenuity. Make walls, doors, and windows from your collected materials, then decorate your fairy house with stones, fallen flowers, acorns, etc. Allow your imagination to run wild as you build the fairy house. This provides an opportunity to express yourself creatively and immerse yourself in a realm of magic. Once complete, it can be nurtured and provide a space for imaginative play at any time. Don't forget to respect the environment by collecting fallen items rather than picking something living and risking disturbing minibeasts.

Make a Time Capsule

This is a perfect way to reflect over and preserve fond memories for the future. It entails making a container filled with personal goods, messages, or keepsakes and burying it to either dig up in years to come or for others to find in the future.

Planning: A little

Age: All ages

Location: Woods, parks, garden

Time: 1–2 hours

Kit list: Sturdy, waterproof container, items to include in the time capsule, sealing materials (tape, glue, etc.), shovel or digging tools

Start by finding a robust and watertight container, such as a metal tin or a plastic box. Choose items that are meaningful to you or symbolise the current period, such as pictures, letters, small keepsakes, or even a written statement about your ambitions and aspirations. Include artefacts that represent your own journey or significant events in your life. Make sure the container can be sealed and is watertight before burying it in the ground and creating a natural marker to find it easily.

Collect or Catch…
Now Let's Cook

Garlicky Goodness

Wild garlic or ramsons (Allium Ursinum) is native to both Europe and Asia and grows in moist woodland. It has been used in cooking for thousands of years. You can pick it for personal use, but it is illegal to dig it up from its roots.

Planning: Not much

Age: All ages

Location: Parks, woodland, gardens

Time: 1–2 hours

Kit list: Basket or bag, water bottle, appropriate clothing and footwear, sunscreen and sunhat (if needed)

Foraging for wild garlic and making yummy cheese and garlic scones is a lovely micro adventure that combines outdoor discovery with culinary creativity!

Make sure you know where to go foraging and when. In the UK, late winter through to early summer is the best time. Pick a bunch of leaves, taking care not to disrupt the plant or remove more than is necessary, as wild garlic is a vital element of the ecology. Head home and find a simple recipe for cheese and garlic scones and serve them with butter or soup.

Tip: If the children like them, you can freeze some scones and pop them in their school lunch box.

Gone Fishing!

This adventure is not just about fishing; it's also about being down by the water's edge, looking for tadpoles, or watching the water's wildlife. You must check local laws on where you can fish, what you can fish for, and if you need a licence.

Planning: Medium

Age: 5+

Location: Rivers, streams, sea, lakes

Time: 2–3 hours or more

Kit list: Fishing rod, fishing line, hooks, bait, fishing tackle box, bucket or cooler for storing fish, fishing net, fishing licence (if required), water bottle, snacks, suitable clothing and footwear, camping chairs, first aid kit, sunhat, hand sanitiser, sunscreen (if needed)

Relax, enjoy the serenity, and wait for a nibble. Remember to observe local fishing restrictions and release the fish, or if you are allowed to keep what you catch, prepare the fish at home for a great supper. If you get children involved in preparing the fish before cooking, they'll be much more likely to try it!

Having the right fishing rod and bait is key. If you are unsure, head to a local fishing equipment shop and ask what you need for the location you plan to visit.

Berry Pie... Yum!

Set off on a berry-picking micro adventure and uncover nature's delectable gifts. Enjoy homemade berry pie or make delicious jam.

Planning: Not much

Age: All ages

Location: Walking trails, footpaths, coastlines, parks, garden

Time: A few hours

Kit list: Basket or container, sun hat, sunscreen, insect repellent, water bottle, appropriate clothing and footwear

Start by researching which berries in your local area you are allowed to pick and can eat. Berries usually grow along roadsides, in woodland, and on coastlines. Research a good location and make sure it's the right time of year.

Berry picking is a great way to connect with nature and relish the tastes of the season, whether you eat them immediately or take them home to prepare a dessert or jam.

Note: For safety, make sure you know what you are picking, and if in any doubt, don't eat it. Blackberries are ideal for collecting and cooking.

Alfresco Dining

There are many skills to learn for building a good fire to cook outdoors, as well as a number of safety considerations. This requires some preparatory thinking about what type of fire to make, where it is safe, and what to cook, but it's all worth the effort as nothing beats cooking and eating outdoors with family and friends. So don't forget to invite others to join you!

Planning: Substantial

Age: All ages

Location: Garden, campsites

Time: Half a day or a full evening

Kit list: Sticks, kindling, tinder, firelighter, rocks, cooking utensils, fireproof gloves, foil or grill grate, cutting board, knife, seasoning, food ingredients, plates, bowls, water, campfire safety equipment, first aid kit

Start by identifying a safe place where you are allowed to have an open fire. The fire needs to be built away from bushes or anything flammable in an open, flat area without overhanging trees. You want to build your fire on a large, flat rock or clear an area of ground, create a large rock circle, and lay a bed of flat sticks in your circle. Now you can gather your fire-making materials. You will need kindling, such as small, dry tree branches, twigs, and chunks of dead tree bark. Next, search for tinder that is dry, fluffy material – dead thistle heads, old man's beard, dried animal poo, cedar bark, and dry grass all work well.

Then you will need to collect fallen, dry, larger sticks for once the fire gets going. Build a nest of kindling, put the tinder inside the nest, and finally, you need a spark to light your fire – matches will do! Three elements are required to make a fire: oxygen, heat, and fuel; this is known as a fire triangle. Remember to never leave a fire unattended by an adult and to have a large bucket of water close by.

Now place a grill or grilling grate over the fire, resting it flat on the rocks, and wait until the flames have gone down so you can cook over hot embers. Cooking over flames will char the food but won't cook it through the middle.

If you would prefer to simplify this adventure and focus more on cooking, you can use an outdoor BBQ instead of building a fire.

Here's a few of my favourite open-fire meals

- Stews and soups
- Chicken, prawn, or veggie skewers
- Hot dogs with fried onions
- Toasted marshmallows
- Whole fish with lemon and butter wrapped in tin foil
- Corn on the cob wrapped in tin foil
- Jacket potatoes with cheese wrapped in tin foil
- Ham, cheese, and spring onion toasties
- Marinated pork chops with butter beans
- Tiroler Gröstl (fried potatoes, onions, bacon, and eggs, season with caraway seeds, paprika, and parsley)

Under the Trees

Wizardry Crafts

Adding a magic theme to your mini adventure provides a compelling reason to hop off the sofa and head out into the wild. No two wands are the same, and different wood brings different powers.

Planning: Not much

Age: 5+

Location: Woodland

Time: 1–2 hours

Kit list: Sun hat, sunscreen, insect repellent, raincoat (if needed), water bottle, comfy clothing and footwear, first aid kit, string, sandpaper, penknife or drawknife, decorative items. Optional: paint

Set the scene before heading out. Read some Harry Potter or watch one of the movies the night before to immerse everyone in the magical mindset.

Head to nearby woodland and search for fallen branches. You can each decide whether to pick a wonky or straight stick. Most types of wood work well; however, keep an eye out for alder, apple, ash, birch, cedar, and elder trees, which all make great wand materials.

Once everyone has found their perfect wand stick, use a penknife or drawknife to peel away the bark. Adults can do this part for younger children. Older children can often do this themselves with safety methods explained and under supervision from an adult. All children can then use sandpaper to smooth off the wood. Now it's time to personalise and decorate your wands. Tie string patterns, stick on charms, paint your wand – it's up to you!

Tip: While everyone is in the mood for magic, consider collecting some fallen items to make a home-brewed potion in a pot in the garden once you return from your expedition.

Build a Den

Ignite a primitive mindset by building a shelter together and promoting teamwork. Autumn is an ideal time to create your den, as you will find fallen-down branches and leaves to build with.

Planning: Not much

Age: All ages

Location: Woodland, garden

Time: Several hours

Kit list: Sun hat, sunscreen, insect repellent, raincoat (if needed) water bottle, snacks, comfy clothing and footwear, first aid kit

For a teepee den, begin by finding a sturdy tree with a fork in the branches that is in easy reach. Next, gather some natural materials to make your den. Look for leaves and branches that have fallen to the ground; don't break off living branches or damage trees. Start by building the frame of the den: rest long, straight sticks in the fork and fan them out around the tree. Cover your den with natural materials, and scatter dried leaves inside to make the ground soft and dry to sit on. Respect the environment by taking the den down at the end of the day and ensuring you leave no trace. If you build your den in the garden, why not replenish everyone's oxygen levels, boost serotonin, and lift the mood by having a campout for the night? When life gets a little hectic, this is a great way to reduce stress levels.

Follow My Lead

Let the children lead this micro adventure by taking turns being the navigator and giving the group directions (e.g., turn clockwise 90 degrees and take 200 steps forward, turn away from the sun and skip for a minute, stop and turn 90 degrees clockwise, walk for 2 minutes, etc.). Take this activity to the woods or a nearby park.

Planning: Not much

Age: All ages

Location: Woods, parks, open space

Time: An hour or two

Kit list: Map or directions, compass, water bottle, snacks, comfortable walking shoes, weather-appropriate clothing, backpack, first aid kit. Optional: camera or smartphone for documenting the adventure

Follow the children's lead and see where their decisions take you. Accept the element of surprise and discovery as you explore new paths and experience unexpected sights and sounds.

Encourage your children to use their imagination. This collaborative micro adventure can teach vital skills like decision-making, cooperation, and spatial awareness. So put your children in charge for a unique, fascinating adventure filled with exploration and togetherness.

Tip: Have a badge to pin on the 'Navigator' and give everyone a turn to lead the group.

Go and Play Walkie-Talkies

Set off on a micro adventure, communicating and navigating across a defined region using walkie-talkies.

Planning: Not much

Age: All ages

Location: Woods, walking trails, parks

Time: 1–2 hours

Kit list: Walkie-talkies, batteries, water bottle, snacks, comfortable walking shoes, weather-appropriate clothing. Optional: map or compass

Assign each group a walkie-talkie and develop a set of communication guidelines. You could create your own code language and write this down as a group before you head out. Explore the environment while keeping connected and exchanging messages. Play exciting games like hide-and-seek, search for a set destination, or navigate the groups back together.

This is a great way to strengthen family relationships and build skills, such as effective communication, problem-solving, and cooperation.

Photo Scavenger Hunt

This simple but exciting adventure involves heading out on a local walking route with a clear task. It's easy for everyone to take part.

Planning: Medium

Age: All ages

Location: Parks, walking trails, woods

Time: 1–2 hours

Kit list: Camera or smartphone, comfortable walking shoes, weather-appropriate clothing, pens, printed pictures of items to find

To prepare, make a list of items you might find on a local walking trail. Next, find pictures online of the items and print out a few coloured copies. Cut them into cards you can take with you on the walk. Head out on a search for all your items, either in small groups or all together. Once you find an item, take a picture and move on to the next item. A photo scavenger hunt stimulates observation and appreciation for the environment around you. So pick up your camera and go on a photo-filled journey that will leave you with beautiful visual memories from your adventure.

Night-Time Adventures

Night Hike with Torches

Go hiking at night with a torch each. As you head out into nature under darkness, you will awaken your senses to the sounds of creatures and marvel at the subtle beauty that emerges from the lunar shadows.

Planning: Medium

Age: 7+

Location: Woodland, parks, walking trails

Time: 1–2 hours

Kit list: Headlamps or torches, comfortable walking shoes, warm clothing, insect repellent, water bottles, snacks, first aid kit, navigation tools (compass, GPS). Optional: hiking poles or walking sticks, camera or smartphone for capturing memories

The night trek provides a distinct viewpoint and a sense of adventure. It's a chance to explore the charm and tranquillity that can only be discovered once the sun goes down. Try some storytelling or stargazing, or simply enjoy the peaceful atmosphere of the night.

Tip: You could turn your walk into a night jog and do it in the rain to create an exhilarating experience. Everyone will sleep soundly after this adventure!

Watch the Moon on the Water

Wait for the perfect clear evening when the stars and moon are bright and in full view to enjoy the mesmerising beauty of the moon reflecting on the water. It will open your thoughts to the grandeur and mystery of the universe around us.

Planning: Not much

Age: 5+

Location: Lakes, rivers, streams, sea

Time: During the night or twilight hours

Kit list: Blanket, warm clothing, snacks, drinks, first aid kit, insect repellent (if needed), torch or headlamp, camping chairs. Optional: binoculars, camera, stargazing or astronomy guidebook, moon phase calendar

Head to a nearby lake or river or down to the sea and find a spot by the water's edge to gaze into the sky and watch the light from the moon glow over the water. This adventure will bring a sense of calm and reflection to the group and provide an opportunity to share stories and food. Take in the fresh night air and enjoy the awe-inspiring majesty of the cosmos.

Search for star constellations, and guide children on how to locate Polaris (the North Star). You do this by finding the Big Dipper (also known as the Plough, the Great Wagon, Saptarishi, and the Saucepan). The two stars on the end of the Dipper's 'cup' point the way to Polaris. Note that if you are in the southern hemisphere, you won't be able to see the North Star.

Remember that safety is paramount. Ensure everyone stays together, and keep children in sight and within reach at all times.

Camp Out for the Night

Sleeping outdoors is amazing for your body, mind, and soul. With plenty of fresh oxygen in your lungs, this experience will boost serotonin levels and brighten your mood. It's also a great stress reliever and can support better sleep. Research where you can camp out in your local area, and then pitch a tent or just roll out your mat. Add more fun to the adventure by inviting friends to join you.

Planning: Medium

Age: All ages

Location: Garden, anywhere that allows wild camping

Time: 1 night

Kit list: Tent, sleeping bags, sleeping mats, pillows, camping chairs, torch, picnic, water bottles, first aid kit, map of the local area, insect repellent, shovel (if needed), clothing appropriate for the weather, personal items (toiletries, medication, etc.), camera or smartphone for capturing memories

Once you've found an appropriate location, pitch your tent (if you prefer to have cover at night), pull out your sleeping bags, and make a pleasant campsite. You could spend the day decorating your camp, finding logs for seats, and creating board games like Noughts and Crosses using sticks and stones for some light entertainment, etc. If the location is suitable and permits fires, you may want to build a campfire (see Alfresco Dining for how to make a good campfire).

Enjoy the serene atmosphere and the sounds of nature as the sun sets. See the night stars and gaze at the wonders of the cosmos overhead. Wake up to beams of light and the fresh, crisp air.

Water Wonders

Life's Amazing on a SUP!

Whether you're a seasoned stand-up paddle boarder (SUP) or watch others and wonder what all the fuss is about, this micro adventure is not to be missed! Paddle boarding is thousands of years old, and the first modern-day paddle board was used in Waikiki in the 1940s. In recent years, it has become one of the most popular water sporting activities, with varying levels of challenge to the sport and diverse environments in which you can take to the water.

> Planning: Medium
>
> Age: 8+
>
> Location: Calm river, canal, ocean, lake
>
> Time: A day
>
> Kit list: Stand-up paddle board (SUP), personal flotation device (PFD), leash, waterproof bag or dry bag, sunscreen, water bottle, snacks, towel, change of clothes, sun hat, sunglasses, water shoes or sandals, safety whistle, first aid kit, navigation tools (map, compass, GPS)

If you are a confident paddle boarder and have good balance and strength, children can sit on the board while you paddle. Note that this takes practice and would only be advised for someone experienced in the sport. As with all water activities, all participants need to be confident in the water and able to swim, and everyone must wear a well-fitted life jacket.

Selecting where to go paddle boarding is a key safety aspect, and if you and the children are new to the sport, you should pick somewhere without tides or strong currents and ideally with low water levels. Choose a wide, slow-flowing river or still lake, and don't go alone; make sure you are in a group or there are other people around. Check where you are allowed to paddle board in your local area, and if you are completely new to this sport, a lesson or two before you go it alone would be highly recommended.

Once you have mastered paddle boarding, you will feel the connection between you, the board, and the water as you balance and manoeuvre through the water. Enjoy the serenity of your surroundings, drink up the sunshine, and marvel at nature. You'll soon realise what all the fuss is about!

Glide on Water

Hiring a canoe or kayak does cost money, but luckily many lakes provide inexpensive rental options. Getting out on the water is a great way to get active, see local wildlife, feel a sense of freedom, and reduce stress. It's also super fun for children and a new skill they can learn.

Planning: Medium

Age: 8+

Location: Lakes, rivers, oceans

Time: A few hours

Kit list: Canoe or kayak, paddles, life jackets, container for belongings, water bottle, snacks, sunscreen, sun hat, sunglasses. Optional: waterproof phone case or dry bag, camera for capturing memories, frisbee, football

This may require some travel to a lake with facilities that rent canoes or kayaks, but it's worth it and is still a relatively low-cost day out. Start by researching where you can go and any restrictions for rental, for example, age, ability, and experience. Make sure to pick a day with low wind and clear skies.

Once you have checked everyone can participate, make sure to call ahead and book. You may want to play some games, such as kayak football, a relay race, or ultimate frisbee. Just check with the rental centre to ensure playing these games is permitted. If not, play a simple game of I-Spy.

Morning Wake-Up Swim

There are numerous studies into the potential health benefits of cold water swimming, as this sport has surged in popularity in recent years. They suggest it can reduce stress, decrease inflammation, improve the immune system, boost self-esteem, give you a natural high as you release endorphins, boost your metabolism, and improve mental health.

> Planning: A little
>
> Age: 10+
>
> Location: Streams, lidos, oceans, lake,
>
> Time: 30 mins to 1 hour
>
> Kit list: Swimwear or wetsuit, buoyancy aids, towel, waterproof sunscreen, water bottle, dry bag, change of clothes, first aid kit. Optional: tow float, swim cap, goggles, swim fins

Start your day with a revitalising dip in the water. This could be a local lido, the sea, a stream, or even a hose or sprinkler in your garden. Pick a local water source where you are allowed to swim that is safe for everyone's ages and abilities. Lidos are great for families with younger children and are less crowded in the early mornings. If you are heading to a local beach, aim for one that has lifeguards. Look at where other people are swimming, read signs, and check the weather forecast and tide timetables. Observe the sea's behaviour first, and identify a safe entry and exit point. Swim along the shore in shallow water. No matter your age or ability, never swim alone. To ease everyone into this activity, start in the summer months and try wearing wetsuits.

Advice, Considerations, and Final Reflections

Top Tips for Family Micro Adventures

- Start children as young as possible.
- Be supportive, not a leader.
- Adapt adventures to suit children's interests and abilities.
- Be environmentally responsible, leave no trace.
- Act as an outdoor role model.
- Encourage exploration and curiosity.
- Always consider safety precautions.
- Pack the right essentials for any trip.
- Have fun and be spontaneous!

Leave No Trace

The 'leave no trace' mindset supports ethical outdoor actions to reduce environmental effects. It stresses keeping natural environments pure and conserving their integrity for future generations. Hiking, camping, backpacking, and other outdoor activities can all be carried out with a 'leave no trace' attitude.

'Leave no trace' is founded on environmental conservation and sustainability. We can assist in safeguarding ecosystems, wildlife habitats, and vulnerable natural resources by reducing the impact we make. This strategy helps conserve the beauty and biological balance of the outdoors, ensuring that others may enjoy and appreciate it in its original condition.

Being environmentally responsible means following the seven key principles of 'leave no trace'.

- Plan ahead and prepare.
- Travel and camp on durable surfaces.
- Waste must be disposed of appropriately.
- Leave what you find.
- Reduce the impact of a campfire.
- Wildlife should be treated with respect.
- Be considerate of others.

To understand more about the 'leave no trace' principles and how to apply them, visit the official Leave No Trace Center for Outdoor Ethics website at https://lnt.org/why/7-principles/. The website offers information, instructional tools, and practical guidance for practising good outdoor ethics.

Explore books, articles, and internet resources to learn more about outdoor ethics, environmental stewardship, and sustainable outdoor behaviours.

Health and Safety Considerations

- **Risk assessment**: Carry out a risk assessment before starting any micro adventure. Identify possible dangers and take appropriate risk-mitigation steps.

- **Equipment and gear**: Ensure you have all the appropriate equipment and gear for the specific micro adventure activity. Consider appropriate clothes, footwear, safety equipment, navigation tools, first aid kits, and emergency communication devices.

- **Physical fitness**: Evaluate your group's fitness level and select micro adventures appropriate for everyone's ability.

- **Weather conditions**: Stay updated about the weather and organise your micro adventure accordingly. Prepare for variations in weather by carrying the right kit, such as rain gear, sunscreen, and insect repellent.

- **Prepare for an emergency**: Be familiar with emergency protocols and know how to respond to an accident or injury.

- **Environmental considerations**: Practise 'leave no trace' principles and respect the environment. Reduce your environmental impact by properly disposing of rubbish and respecting animals and natural ecosystems.

- **Personal safety**: Stay attentive, observe safety standards, and be aware of any hazards in your surroundings.

- **Group dynamics**: Maintain strong communication and collaboration when engaging in a group micro adventure. Take care of one another and follow safety rules.

- **Training and education**: Any activities from this book are carried out at your own risk. If you don't feel confident that you or others participating have the skills to complete a particular activity safely, take a class that can give you and others these skills, or get advice from someone with more experience.

- **Maintenance**: Maintain your equipment regularly to ensure its safety and dependability.

All good things are wild and free.

– Henry David Thoreau

Printed in Great Britain
by Amazon

29804536R00050